Praise for *Recovery*

"'The lungs are the seat of grief,' J. L. Conrad's *Recovery* begins. I see this brilliant sequence demonstrating a similar process—of flux and transformation, of expansion and contraction, of taking in and letting go—as our speaker embarks on a new journey in the wake of loss. I admire the way Conrad manipulates language to compose and recompose a scene, reminding me of Simone Weil's declaration that 'absolutely unmixed attention is prayer.' These poems skillfully pair the surreal—the wish-fulfillment and diorama-building of dreams—with remnants of the everyday. They turn, they stumble, they play sleight of hand, they startle us awake. With a lyrical vision so precise it reaches wildness, *Recovery* opens up new realities in the aftermath of loss."

—Gale Marie Thompson

"In *Recovery*, J. L. Conrad weaves story, memory, dream, history, and more, into a meditation on family and the place of a self among others. It's an always elusive subject, fraught with protection spells and a necessary vulnerability that allows the reader full participation in the various emergencies of the present and it keeps coming at us, in, as Conrad writes, 'Criticism is talking about art // behind its back. Consider this a missive / from the front.'"

—John Gallaher

RECOVERY

A POEM

Library of Congress Cataloging-in-Publication Data

Names: Conrad, J. L., 1975- author.
Title: Recovery : poems / J. L. Conrad.
Description: First edition. | Huntsville : TRP: The University Press
of SHSU, [2023] | "A Robert Phillips Poetry Chapbook Prize."
Identifiers: LCCN 2022039147 (print) | LCCN 2022039148
(ebook) | ISBN
  9781680033403 (paperback) | ISBN 9781680033410 (ebook)
Subjects: LCSH: Loss (Psychology)—Poetry. | Grief—Poetry. |
  Consolation—Poetry. | LCGFT: Poetry.
Classification: LCC PS3603.O556 R43 2023 (print) | LCC
PS3603.O556
  (ebook) | DDC 811/.6—dc23/eng/20220819
LC record available at https://lccn.loc.gov/2022039147
LC ebook record available at https://lccn.loc.gov/2022039148

Cover design by Bradley Alan Ivey
Cover image licensed via Shutterstock.com
Interior design by Miranda Ramírez
Printed and bound in the United States of America

Published by TRP: The University Press of SHSU
Huntsville, Texas 77341
texasreviewpress.org

RECOVERY

A POEM

J. L. Conrad

TRP: The University Press of SHSU
Huntsville, Texas

◖ ◖ ◖

The lungs are the seat of grief,

she tells me. Also something
about a vanishing twin.

It is why, she explains, you have
a hard time with

closed doors. And do you
ever feel yourself in a room, talking

and then someone picking up
the threads of your words

and casting them out
again? Like slipping on a cloak.

For some organs to heal
she says, it takes years. In the mean-

time the house blooms with heat.

◐ ◐ ◐

This, the place
from where it all started.

We go out and back and still
the loops of our hands around each other.

Leaves flashing their underparts.
A house in the trees.

Truth be told, I have never dreamed
of becoming animal.

We go out and back and still
the bones of our hands.

◐ ◐ ◐

In the dream I was heading

to band practice, clarinet
in a handbag, my father

at the wheel of the pickup. He was taking
the long way through town,

its square filled with those tending
wheeled stretchers with

bodies on them. Further on, others
jumped at a leisurely pace

from the mouth of a charred building
onto the surface of a trampoline.

Whole blocks had burned, but
we made it back onto the highway,

clarinet clanking furiously.

○ ○ ○

We looked at each other, and
in that space it's not like

I had anything better to do.
As it turned out, that was the last time

we saw each other. Unless you count

the dream in which I showed up
wearing your shirt, as if

you had claimed me, and yet
the person who looked like you from the back

turned and I remembered
that you had died.

◐ ◐ ◐

The moon, in my dream, is called
the otter moon: egg-shaped, like

one sitting with his back
to the view. A shrapnel of light.

By which I mean shards—
water broken and breaking. Lake's surface

crazed, the ice gone. Suitcases
surround us, a geometry of surfaces,

one of them ready
to bring the whole thing down.

Imagine your pain as an animal.
Skillful adversary hiding

under a log, in a cave.
What color is it?

○ ○ ○

She said you can plan
on keeping your teeth. She said

your teeth will continue to move, to edge
themselves sideways.

Let's stop them in their tracks.
Let's break apart the battlements.

○ ○ ○

Lately we've taken to
complaining of assassins,

their ropes and sneaky ways,
how we never see them coming, even

when moon sheds its light
in the passageways.

Blood winging to a shoreline.
Mute, like *mule*—the consonants

of hooves clopping, shearing
sound from silence.

This go-round the only one—
or not: my son saying *when I die*

and grow up again, as if a fact, and then
the question—*will I have brown skin?*

and then *but how will we know*
each other? And my answer:

I will always know you.

❂ ❂ ❂

Last night's dream:
a child, a balcony, a barn floor.

It was a dangerous child.
The barn floor was red.

The balcony leaned over.
Most of my dreams

involve houses
into which I might move.

Items I have put "somewhere safe"
and cannot be found.

◐ ◐ ◐

The poles in the river signify
places where it is possible

to fall through limestone
into a cave or cavern beneath. One might

land up to one's waist in water
or disappear entirely.

Each a distinct possibility.

○ ○ ○

Waiting in the wings, I thought
to buy peanut butter but not get it on my skin or hair.

The grocery store still hadn't closed, even though
plans had been made to do so.

They are giving up on the beehives.
Who is *they* some will ask.

The car floating back toward me.
The others hightailing it out.

o o o

I do not have a nametag or, if I do, it says
"Alternate, bumped in," as in

"the one not chosen." What is the opposite
of "the chosen one"?

All of this relates to the ancient thing observed here (liver)
    in relation to being an employee
    in relation to being a child of God
    not between secular and religious
    but between two versions of faith.

I have released that for you, she says.

○ ○ ○

I am interested in meat and
the woman sitting in the middle of it all

on the bodies, doing needlepoint,
the silver fish of her needle.

◐ ◐ ◐

It's as though your whole body
is twisted, she says.

A spiral from the bottom of your neck
through your spine.

The parable is not the parabolic
though both do have curve, have landslide.

You might need to live with a certain
degree of pain, she says.

* * *

My son and I pretend the sand along the curb
is quicksand, the fire hydrants

dragons, the branches we find
along the way magic wands.

The trees produce crabapples
and small, profuse flowers.

The trees are candles.
I am not used to making such concessions.

Such amens, such amendments.
Spring with its fangs and blossoms.

○ ○ ○

Do you want transformation?
What do you want to be done?

I want a dog to be a dog.
I want to be a dog a dog.

I want to write the whole thing
backward. What was it

I wanted in the end?
This is all, in one way or another,

a conversation about the untranslatable.
The scream but not the horror.

We are losing something
in every moment.

What is the problem?
Birds unsettling the marshes.

Blood waging its wars.
Desertification has its hands on you.

◐ ◐ ◐

I did not know what to expect
this morning, or any other morning

in fact. Yet I have had
two conversations in one day

about the one who followed. The body
that is and isn't a body.

It's important to keep your heart
meridian open, she tells me.

Maybe praise or the lack of it
is part of the problem.

If it's a real mystery, then it will
hold water.

○ ○ ○

I'm thinking of abandonment.
Or unabandonment.

How we rarely cast ashore.
Waves spitting us out.

Where you go, I will.
It occurs to me that maybe

we are speaking about transference.
Unraveling the prayer to its roots.

Paring it back to the core.

We hold hands and
blow out the candle.

o o o

Criticism is talking about art

behind its back. Consider this a missive
from the front.

Consider this the front, trailing
clouds. They have invented

a new kind of cloud, or a new name
for existing clouds, the second being

more likely. Like being underwater
some have said. Insert Latin name here.

Insert self into landscape, between
the horses and the too-still pond.

Your voice the opposite of hurricane.

● ● ●

The skeleton of the clothesline.

Put those words back
where they came from—

don't just leave them there

like Easter eggs
for someone else to pick up.

We thought we knew
the answers. The tree

we did not mean to cut down—

and would have kept
in the end, the way

we cut out the roofedge to
accommodate the other's trunk.

Harrow the soul.
Rouse the hackles, the shackles.

Let's see what happens from here.

Something else is going on.
Something is wrong.

There are ways to undo
what has been done.

I'm thinking about something
and it is this: I don't know

that you're the right person
for the job.

It was a reaction against settlement.
We're not going to talk about it.

The way green wood doesn't burn

and how the winter stores
were set alight.

I have another question
about how it all works.

○ ○ ○

Reading as a form of.
The ghost of milk.

What does it mean to hold
one's body "like a dancer"?

What color is your moral compass?
Does your imaginary friend
have a dog?

A dismissive from the front.
A shelving of intent.

A cavalcade, a barrage.

The barracks shed dust
at their seams.

A thousand miles away, water
from which it is not possible
to see shoreline.

But do we have permission to bury our dead.

Yes I do understand
what I am asking.

o o o

In my dream we were in a tree
and we were suffering. In this case,

suffering *with* could not alleviate
suffering. It proved impossible to overlook

the pits in our stomachs.

The car lurched forward, into the knees
of the pedestrian, the line of pilgrims.

❍ ❍ ❍

I have a tendency to exaggerate
the obvious. To make amends.

I had forgotten where I started and yet
I didn't want to begin the maze again.

Someone mentioned a book
and also eating. Someone else confessed

waiting outside the gates and feeling
bad about it. Are we

moving in any direction at all?

The dumb soup of the body,
its preponderance to endure.

○ ○ ○

Such pedestrian urges.

I wonder what
we were thinking. Could someone

please reconstruct the scene

from the ground up,
paint its backdrop?

We will not stand for it
is what I mean to say.

◐ ◐ ◐

This is not metaphor
but something different.

Not the scream but the horror.
Not the charm but the mystery.

Has anyone else noticed
the disco ball suspended overhead?

Could you please name and number
the uses of the infinite?

I am on a journey
and something is missing.

Are you bored yet? Please
reframe your question.

o o o

In complete darkness, by which I mean
incomplete darkness, as always here—

the hard-edged bowl of the lake.

Someone might say *chalice*.
Some might say *sword*.

○ ○ ○

Let us lead language there to drink.
Let us circumpose the wreckage

created by all those shining knives.
The expected deaths.

The professors of warfare
studied the long advance.

It is always happening somewhere
else. Beside the point.

Behind the fortifications.
It's like forgetting how to swim.

Or having forgotten.
The better to understand you with.

Should I add *my dear*.

○ ○ ○

We are looking for ways around it,
to tell the story differently.

Everyone called to the windows
pressed up against them

to witness
the six wild turkeys

in their parade line
now heading back to the trees.

This is not how it ends.
Let this not be how it ends.

o o o

In my dream I touched his arm.
He was overdressed for the event

as were his companions.

We were all on a beachhead.
He did not know me—

or should I say recognize—

but drew me into a hug nonetheless,
his companions watching.

Later in the crowd, someone

placed his hand on my breastbone,
a blessing. They were glad

to see me go, the interruption vanish.

How to translate the light
that hits the eye the camera.

○ ○ ○

Lately I've been thinking about
emergency versus emergence.

The way we are always on a cusp.
It is nice to think dreams

might speak some truths to us.
If we are all still here.

The body slips its moorings.

It is a voice and
a voice waiting for you.

I dreamed, he said, that you
did not have a head and

were still dancing.

Notes and Acknowledgments

This long poem was written during a one-week period in April 2017 and, in part, offers a response to G.C. Waldrep's book *Testament* and a talk that he gave on April 7 at "Reimagining the Sacred & the Cool: A Literary Symposium," held in Madison, WI.

"The scream but not the horror" comes from Francis Bacon's interviews with David Sylvester in *The Brutality of Fact* as related in a talk by Anne Carson at Dia:Beacon in June 2005.

"The poles in the river" recounts a conversation with the poet Todd Davis.

"The one who followed" is Thomas from the Biblical Gospel of John.

Among other associations, the phrase "Where you go, I will" reflects Ruth's words to her mother Naomi in the Biblical book of Ruth.

"They have invented / a new kind of cloud" denotes *undulatus asperatus*, the first addition to the *International Cloud Atlas* in over half a century.

"The barracks shed dust / at their seams" refers to the 2017 Shayrat missile strike by the U.S. in Syria.

I am indebted to the friends, family members, and healing professionals who have supported me over the years. Some conversations with them are reflected in this material although, because memory is imperfect, attribution to specific individuals is often not possible. Any misrecollections or misinterpretations remain entirely my own.

My deepest appreciation goes out to Texas Review Press, its editors and staff, and to contest judge Taylor Johnson for believing in this work and selecting it for publication.

Parts of *Recovery* first appeared, sometimes in slightly different form, in the following journals, which I gratefully acknowledge:

The Laurel Review
  "Lately we've taken to / complaining of assassins..."
  "The moon, in my dream, is called / the otter moon: egg-
      shaped, like..."
  "Do you want transformation? / What do you want to be
      done?"
  "Reading as a form of. / The ghost of milk."
  "This is not metaphor / but something different."
  "Lately I've been thinking about / emergency versus
      emergence."

Jellyfish
  "The lungs are the seat of grief..."
  "In complete darkness, by which I mean..."
  "Let us lead language there to drink..."
  "It's as though your whole body..."
  "I'm thinking of abandonment..."